THIS BOOK BELONGS TO

Name: Age:

Favourite player:

2021/2022

My Predictions...	Actual...

The Canaries' final position:

The Canaries' top scorer:

Premier League winners:

Premier League top scorer:

FA Cup winners:

EFL Cup winners:

Contributors: Simon Larkins, Peter Rogers

A TWOCAN PUBLICATION

©2021. Published by twocan under licence from Norwich City Football Club.

Every effort has been made to ensure the accuracy of information within this publication but the publishers cannot be held responsible for any errors or omissions. Views expressed are those of the authors and do not necessarily represent those of the publishers or the football club. All rights reserved.

ISBN: 978-1-913362-97-3

PICTURE CREDITS:
Norwich City FC, Matthew Usher, Matthew Brasnett, Alamy, Reuters, Press Association.

£10

LOTUS
LOTUS

CONTENTS

2021/22 SQUAD

1 TIM KRUL

POSITION: Goalkeeper

DOB: 03/04/1988

COUNTRY: Netherlands

Dutch international goalkeeper Tim Krul has been in exceptional form since signing for Norwich City on the eve of the 2018/19 season. In the 2019/20 season he was voted the Canaries' player of the season and last campaign he was, again, a key player as Norwich won the Championship with a record points haul. Known for his penalty saving heroics, Tim has represented the Netherlands at the 2014 World Cup, saving crucial penalties in a quarter-final shootout victory over Costa Rica.

2 MAX AARONS

POSITION: Defender

DOB: 04/01/2000

COUNTRY: England

A product of Norwich City's Academy, Max Aarons is widely regarded as one of the most talented right-backs in the country. He made his debut for the club in an East Anglian derby away at Portman Road and has not looked back since. Last season he was an almost ever-present in the team, playing more minutes than any other player, as the club secured a record points total and their second Championship title in three years.

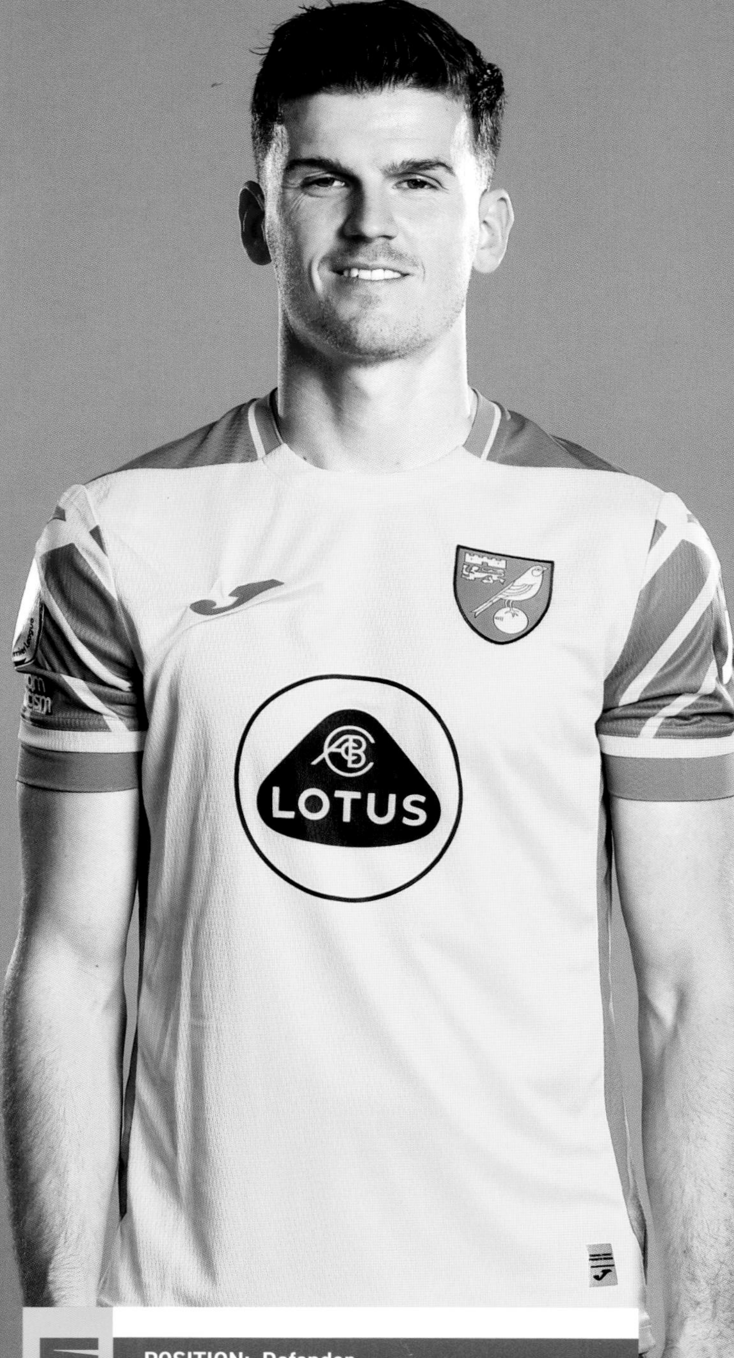

3 SAM BYRAM

POSITION: Defender

DOB: 16/09/1993

COUNTRY: England

Full-back Sam Byram joined the Canaries from West Ham United in the summer of 2019 and played his first game for the club as Norwich secured a memorable 3-2 victory over Manchester City at Carrow Road. Sam, who featured 20 times in all competitions for City in the 2019/20 season, can play at right-back or left-back. However, he did not feature for the Canaries last season because of injury.

4 BEN GIBSON

POSITION: Defender

DOB: 15/01/1993

COUNTRY: England

Central defender Ben Gibson signed a permanent deal at Norwich City in the summer, having initially signed on a season-long loan from Premier League Burnley in September 2020. Ben had a superb first season with Norwich, making 29 appearances in all competitions until an ankle injury curtailed his campaign in late March. By that point his leadership, both on and off the pitch, had put the team on the verge of promotion to the Premier League.

5 GRANT HANLEY

POSITION: Defender

DOB: 20/11/1991

COUNTRY: Scotland

City skipper Grant Hanley featured in 44 games for Norwich last season, marshalling the defence superbly with his speed and aggression. Grant, who signed for Norwich in August 2017, came second in the fans' vote for the player of the season award and netted a crucial goal in a 2-1 away win at Cardiff. The Scottish international also represented his country in the summer at Euro 2020.

6 CHRISTOPH ZIMMERMANN

POSITION: Defender

DOB: 12/01/1993

COUNTRY: Germany

Christoph Zimmermann has been a popular member of the Norwich City team since following head coach Daniel Farke from Borussia Dortmund II to Norwich City in the summer of 2017. A brave defender, Christoph missed only six games in the club's 2018/19 Championship-winning campaign before competing, and captaining the team, in the Premier League. He played 22 games last season as the club won the Championship again.

7 LUKAS RUPP

POSITION: Midfielder

DOB: 08/01/1991

COUNTRY: Germany

Having played for Stuggart and Hoffenheim in the Bundesliga, Lukas Rupp joined the Canaries in January 2020. A central midfielder who is comfortable in attacking roles, Lukas played 12 games for Norwich in our last Premier League season and then 25 games as the club achieved promotion back to the Premier League in 2020/21. He was a key figure, dictating play from the base of the midfield.

8 BILLY GILMOUR

POSITION: Midfielder

DOB: 11/06/2001

COUNTRY: Scotland

Young Scottish midfielder Billy Gilmour joined Norwich City on a season-long loan deal in July. He was part of the Chelsea squad that lifted the Champions League last season and made 22 appearances for the London club that campaign. He also impressed in a Scotland shirt at Euro 2020, picking up the man of the match award in the country's 0-0 draw with England at Wembley.

10 KIERAN DOWELL

POSITION: Midfielder

DOB: 10/10/1997

COUNTRY: England

Attacking midfielder Kieran Dowell joined Norwich City at the start of last season, following a number of successful loan spells from Everton to Championship sides Nottingham Forest, Sheffield United, Derby County and Wigan Athletic. Kieran netted on his Norwich City debut against Luton Town and scored six goals in 26 appearances in his first season at the club as the team won promotion to the Premier League.

11 PRZEMYSŁAW PŁACHETA

POSITION: Midfielder

DOB: 23/03/1998

COUNTRY: Poland

Blessed with phenomenal pace, Polish international Przemysław Płacheta arrived at Norwich City in July 2020 from Śląsk Wrocław. He scored his first goal for Norwich City in a 2-2 draw against Preston North End on September 19 and played a total of 28 games in all competitions for the club in the 2020/21 season.

14 TODD CANTWELL

POSITION: Midfielder

DOB: 27/02/1998

COUNTRY: England

Norfolk-born midfielder Todd Cantwell graduated from the club's academy, making his league debut against Reading in September 2018. That season he played 27 games in all competitions and the following campaign he played 37 games in the Premier League, netting six times including in a famous home win over Manchester City. Last season he was, again, a key player in the side netting in crucial victories over Sheffield Wednesday and Cardiff City as Norwich City secured promotion.

15 OZAN KABAK

POSITION: Defender

DOB: 25/03/2000

COUNTRY: Turkey

Turkish defender Ozan Kabak joined Norwich City in August, on a season-long loan from FC Schalke 04 in August. Born in the Turkish capital of Ankara, Ozan began his career with Galatasaray, before then moving to Germany to sign for VfB Stuttgart in a four-and-a-half-year deal. In his first season in the Bundesliga he won the Rookie of the Season award and in June 2019 he moved to Schalke. He then played 14 games in the Bundesliga last season, before he joined an injury-hit Liverpool in February 2021, where he played 13 times for the Reds in the Premier League.

17 MILOT RASHICA

POSITION: Midfielder

DOB: 28/06/1996

COUNTRY: Kosovo

Milot Rashica became a Norwich City player in June 2021, signing from Werder Bremen for an undisclosed fee. The Kosovo international was an in-demand player following three impressive seasons in the Bundesliga. He played 100 games for Werder scoring 27 goals. At international level Milot represented Albania twice at full international level, before announcing in August 2016 that he was switching to Kosovo, after the country was accepted into UEFA and FIFA competitions that year.

16 MATHIAS NORMANN

POSITION: Midfielder

DOB: 28/05/1996

COUNTRY: Norway

Defensive midfielder Mathias Normann completed a season-long loan move to Norwich City with an option to buy in August 2021. The Norwegian began his senior career in 2012 at Lofoten, before playing for Bodø/Glimt in the top flight. In the summer of 2017, Brighton & Hove Albion brought Mathias to England for the first time, however he was only able to feature for their Under-23s side. Brighton sent Mathias on loan to Molde, where he totalled 18 appearances in all competitions under Ole Gunnar Solskjaer. Ahead of the 2018/19 season, he then completed a permanent move to Rostov, who were competing in the Russian Premier League. He made a total of 52 appearances for the club across three seasons.

18 CHRISTOS TZOLIS

POSITION: Striker

DOB: 30/01/2002

COUNTRY: Greece

Christos Tzolis is a winger who can also play up front. He moved to Norwich City with an impressive strike rate, having scored 16 goals in 46 matches for Greek Super League side PAOK last season, including goals in European matches against Beşiktaş, AEL and PSV Eindhoven. Last season he helped PAOK to finish second in the Super League and win the Greek cup. He has also been capped by Greece at international level.

19 JACOB SØRENSEN

POSITION: Midfielder

DOB: 03/03/1998

COUNTRY: Denmark

Danish midfielder Jacob Sørensen is a versatile and reliable member of the Norwich City squad. Despite being right-footed and having played much of his career in midfield, Jacob spent the majority of last season performing admirably at left-back. He was thrown into that position away at Brentford, following an injury to Xavi Quintillá in the warm up, but excelled and played 20 games before returning to his normal midfield berth.

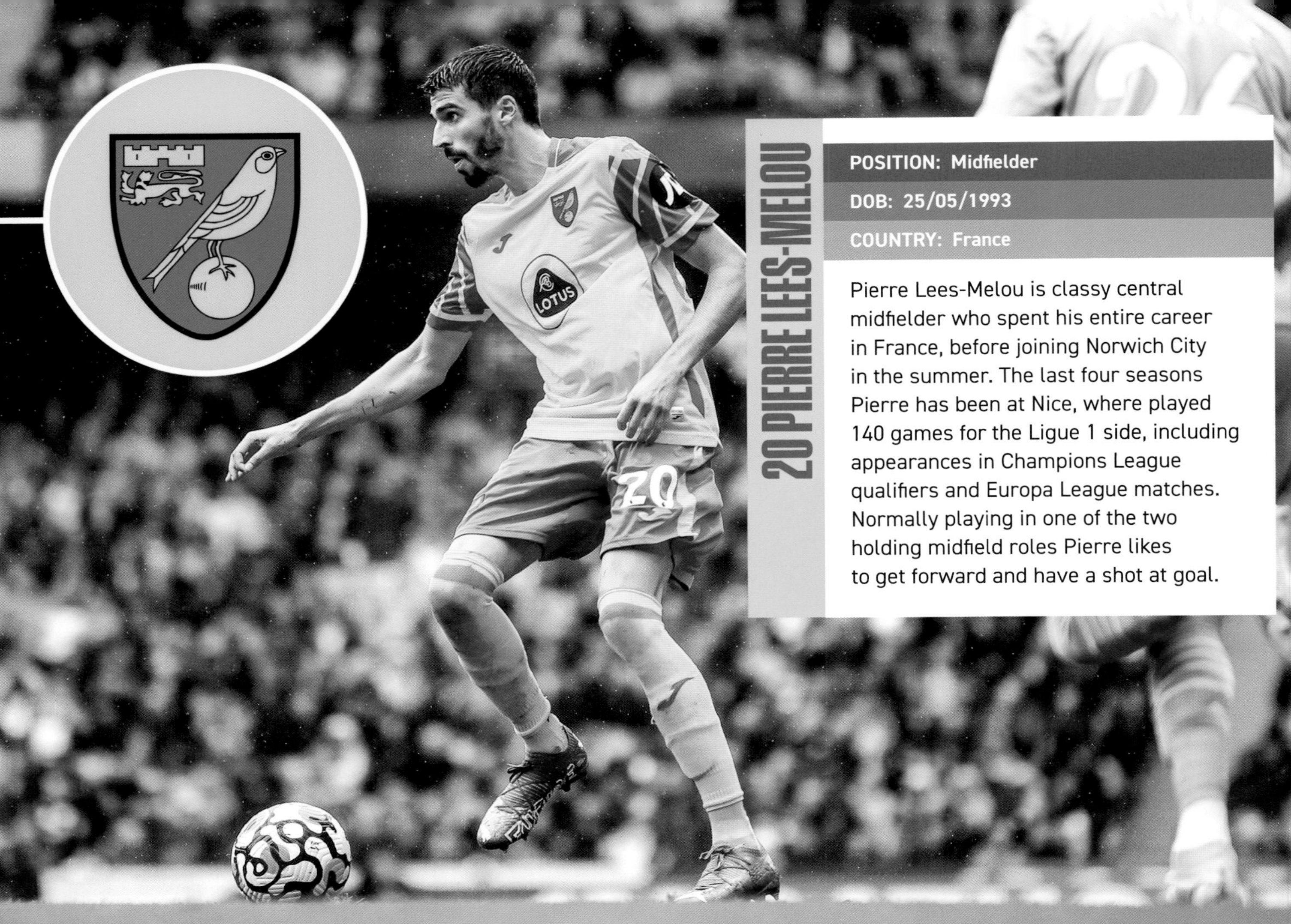

20 PIERRE LEES-MELOU

POSITION: Midfielder

DOB: 25/05/1993

COUNTRY: France

Pierre Lees-Melou is classy central midfielder who spent his entire career in France, before joining Norwich City in the summer. The last four seasons Pierre has been at Nice, where played 140 games for the Ligue 1 side, including appearances in Champions League qualifiers and Europa League matches. Normally playing in one of the two holding midfield roles Pierre likes to get forward and have a shot at goal.

21 BRANDON WILLIAMS

POSITION: Defender

DOB: 03/09/2000

COUNTRY: England

Norwich City completed the season-long loan signing of 20-year-old full-back Brandon Williams from Manchester United at the start of the 2021/22 Premier League season. Brandon joined Manchester United's academy in 2017, and made his first team debut when he was brought on during a Carabao Cup game against Rochdale in 2019. Across the Premier League, Champions League, Europa League, FA Cup and Carabao Cup, Brandon has now made a total of 50 appearances for Manchester United. They included a UEFA Europa League semi-final second leg away to AS Roma, in which he played the full 90 minutes at right-back.

22 TEEMU PUKKI

POSITION: Striker

DOB: 29/03/1990

COUNTRY: Finland

Finnish international Teemu Pukki has been firing in goals for Norwich City for the past three seasons. He hit the back of the net 29 times as the club was promoted from the Championship in 2018/19 and then added 11 Premier League goals to his name the campaign after. Last season he netted 26 times in 41 games. He also scored 10 goals to help Finland qualify for their first major tournament in Euro 2020.

23 KENNY McLEAN

POSITION: Midfielder

DOB: 08/01/1992

COUNTRY: Scotland

Kenny McLean has been at the heart of the Norwich City midfield for the past two seasons, making 42 appearances during the club's 2019/20 Premier League campaign and playing 39 games during the Championship title winning campaign of 2020/21. Playing at the base of the midfield Kenny has proved good a breaking up play as well as finding a killer assist for those in front of him.

24 JOSH SARGENT

POSITION: Striker

DOB: 20/02/2000

COUNTRY: USA

Josh Sargent signed for Norwich City in the summer from Bundesliga side Werder Bremen. Capped by the United States at international level 16 times, Josh became the fifth youngest goalscorer in the country's history when he netted against Bolivia in 2018. Known for his impressive work rate, Josh scored seven goals in 35 games for Werder last season.

26 BALI MUMBA

POSITION: Defender

DOB: 08/10/2001

COUNTRY: England

Highly rated youngster Bali Mumba joined the Canaries in the summer of 2020, from Sunderland. The full-back, who can also play in midfield, has represented England at all age groups from under-16 to under-19. He made his debut for Norwich City last season in an EFL Cup defeat to Luton and made his first league appearance as a second half substitute in a 3-1 win over Bristol City.

28 ANGUS GUNN

POSITION: Goalkeeper

DOB: 22/01/1996

COUNTRY: England

Son of legendary Norwich City keeper Bryan Gunn, Angus sealed a return to his boyhood club in June. Angus was born in Norfolk and progressed through the academy before moving to Manchester City. He would return to Carrow Road on loan for the 2017/18 season, playing every single league match in Daniel Farke's first season in charge. After returning to the Etihad, Angus was then sold to Southampton where he spent three seasons before securing a permanent move back to Norwich.

30 DIMITRIS GIANNOULIS

POSITION: Defender

DOB: 17/10/1995

COUNTRY: Greece

Left-back Dimitris Giannoulis joined Norwich City in January 2021 from PAOK. The Greek international arrived in England with a reputation for being an attack minded full back and he didn't disappoint providing several assists and dangerous balls into the box during the final 16 games of the campaign. He has been capped at full international level by Greece and has also won the Greek Super League and Greek Cup during his career.

33 MICHAEL MCGOVERN

POSITION: Goalkeeper

DOB: 12/07/1984

COUNTRY: Northern Ireland

Experienced Northern Ireland international goalkeeper Michael McGovern played a few games last season filling in for Tim Krul when he was injured. A star performer for Northern Ireland, Michael played a major role in his country's qualification for the finals of Euro 2016 and their success in reaching the knockout stages. He signed for Norwich in 2016, following spells at Celtic, Ross County, Falkirk and Hamilton Academicals.

35 ADAM IDAH

POSITION: Striker

DOB: 11/02/2001

COUNTRY: Republic Of Ireland

Having announced his arrival in the first team with an FA Cup hat-trick against Preston North End in January 2020, Adam Idah then went on to make several Premier League appearances before representing his country at full international level in September 2020. He then scored the opening goal of the club's 2020/21 Championship campaign away at Huddersfield, before going on to net other goals away at Wycombe Wanderers and Barnsley during the title winning campaign.

44 ANDREW OMOBAMIDELE

POSITION: Defender

DOB: 23/06/2002

COUNTRY: Republic Of Ireland

Making his first start for Norwich City away at Preston North End in April 2021, Andrew Omobamidele helped the club to promotion to the Premier League with three clean sheets from the final eight games of the season. Composed in possession and strong in the air, Andrew received his first call up to the Republic of Ireland senior squad in the summer for friendlies against Andorra and Hungary.

JOSH SARGENT

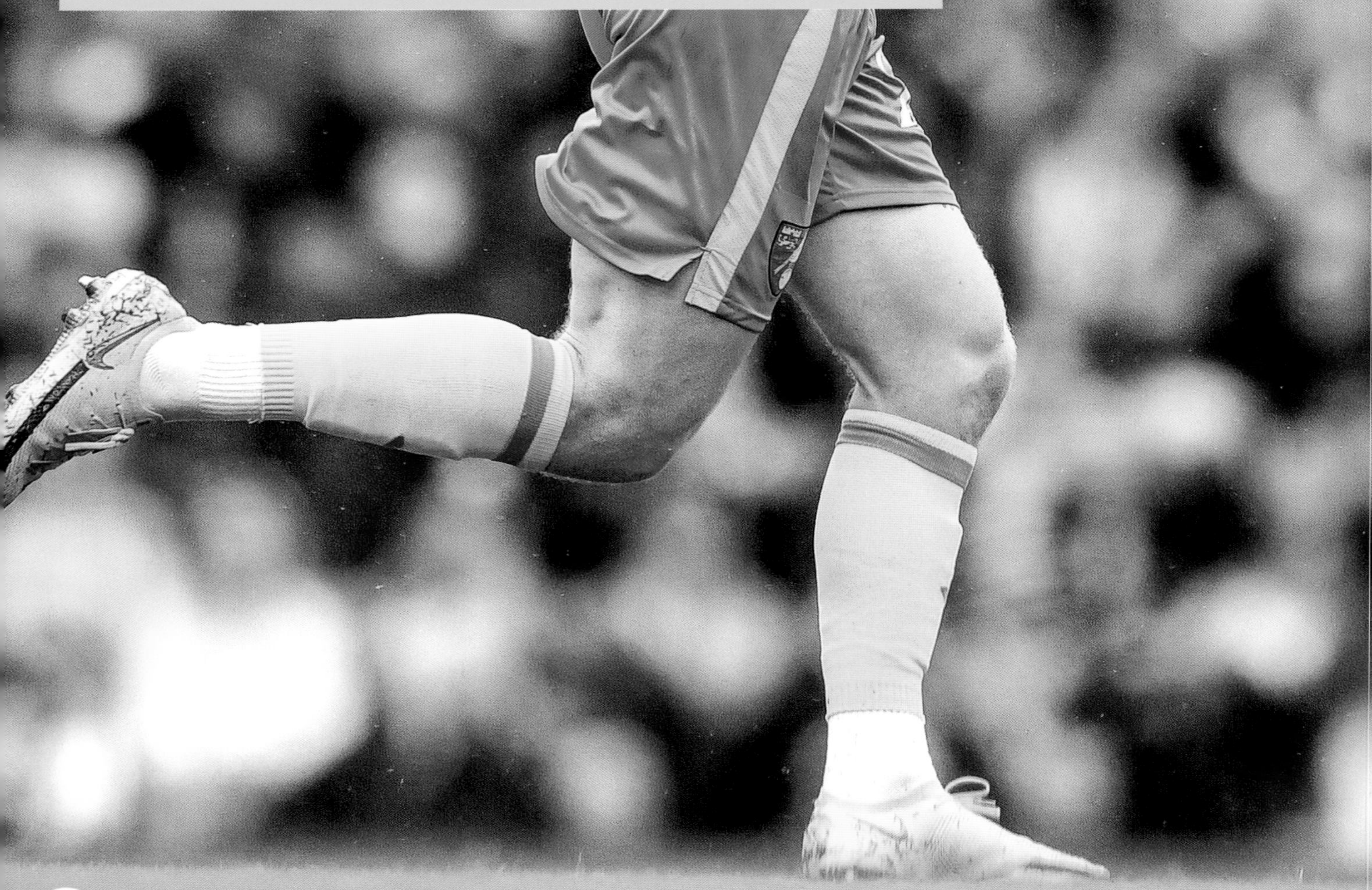

SIDE-FOOT PASS

The side-foot pass is one of the most accurate passing techniques over shorter distances. The ability to find one of your teammates with a pass, even when under severe pressure, and retain possession of the ball is an essential factor in the way the game is played today.

SOCCER SKILLS

EXERCISE ONE

Set up a 10 x 10m grid. In one corner there are two players and on each of the other three corners there is one player.

Player A starts with the ball. Each player must pass the ball round the square in sequence then follow their pass. A passes to B then runs after his pass and takes up B's starting position. B passes to C and follows his pass to take C's position, and so on. All of the players must control the ball then pass it with the inside of their foot.

Key Factors

1. **Non-kicking foot alongside the ball.**
2. **Pass with the inside of the foot.**
3. **Strike through the middle of the ball.**
4. **Keep your eyes on the ball and your head steady.**

EXERCISE TWO

The set up is the same as exercise one.

In this exercise the players pass the ball in sequence, A through to D, but do not follow their pass, remaining stationary.

As soon as A plays the first pass, E sets off racing around the outside of the starting point. The players must pass the ball as quickly and accurately as possible while under pressure from E, who cannot tackle but is effectively racing the ball round the square.

The same key factors apply in this exercise as in the first, but the players are required to be able to pass the ball accurately while under pressure.

Any team who can retain possession through good accurate passing will always make it very difficult for the opposition. The side-foot pass is one of the most accurate passing techniques.

Goalkeeper Bryan Gunn arrived at Carrow Road in October 1986 following a £100,000 transfer from Aberdeen. Over the next 12 years he amassed 477 appearances for the club and became one of the most popular players to represent the club.

An outstanding shot stopper, Bryan controlled his area with authority and was also comfortable with the ball at his feet. His performances twice saw him collect the Barry Butler Memorial Trophy as the club's Player of the Season.

A key player in Mike Walker's 1992/93 side that battled for the Premier League title - Bryan played in all six of the club's UEFA Cup fixtures the following season.

CANARIES HEROES

BRYAN GUNN

HANDS

Blessed with the ability to quickly bring his hands into action to repel the opposition's efforts on goal, Bryan could always be relied upon to pull off saves and use his hands effectively to either gather the ball or push it to safety.

FEET

The modern day goalkeeper needs to be comfortable with the ball at his feet and Bryan really was ahead of his time in that respect. In 1992 when a rule change prevented goalkeepers picking up back-passes from teammates, Bryan's impressive ability to play the ball with his feet really came to the fore.

EYES

Always keeping a close eye on the ball, goalkeeper Bryan used his sight to judge the flight of crosses and the speed of shots heading his way. Sight is such a vital part of goalkeeping particularly when quickly assessing whether to come for a ball or leave it for a defender.

VOICE

Charged with organising the defensive unit in front of him, goalkeeper Bryan would often he heard barking instructions to his teammates. With the whole pitch in his sight it is an important part of the goalkeeper's role to advise teammates of the dangers he can spot.

ALL OF THESE FOOTY TERMS ARE HIDDEN IN THE GRID, EXCEPT FOR ONE... CAN YOU WORK OUT WHICH ONE?

A	G	F	G	O	L	D	E	N	G	O	A	L	A	A	V	C	U	R	B
O	C	L	E	A	N	S	H	E	E	T	N	T	X	O	A	S	A	E	V
D	R	I	B	B	L	I	N	G	A	Y	H	B	L	U	C	A	T	M	I
E	B	P	H	R	N	R	U	T	F	F	Y	U	R	C	V	N	S	O	F
A	F	F	H	I	T	T	H	E	W	O	O	D	W	O	R	K	M	J	G
D	I	L	C	E	N	S	X	D	T	V	R	C	G	R	G	E	O	T	S
B	M	A	D	J	P	Z	E	U	I	W	J	F	N	E	A	D	E	Z	M
A	R	P	K	U	L	I	E	F	S	B	M	A	M	P	I	K	O	S	R
L	Q	A	T	A	T	M	S	D	O	E	M	T	R	P	J	P	Q	P	A
L	Y	V	C	P	O	A	G	O	I	D	U	A	A	I	Y	T	N	B	I
S	I	W	U	E	T	G	T	A	R	N	V	B	T	K	A	H	V	W	N
P	R	C	L	I	N	I	C	A	L	F	I	N	I	S	H	E	R	N	B
E	R	Z	N	S	T	C	H	X	M	A	M	A	M	I	E	N	L	A	O
C	Q	E	H	C	N	S	H	Y	O	S	U	J	G	L	T	U	E	M	W
I	O	A	F	O	S	P	T	E	W	R	O	D	B	Z	A	M	X	T	K
A	J	I	N	F	F	O	X	I	N	T	H	E	B	O	X	B	F	E	I
L	K	A	D	E	A	N	T	Y	V	N	R	K	B	S	Q	I	C	G	C
I	M	G	F	M	U	G	I	A	N	T	K	I	L	L	I	N	G	R	K
S	X	P	B	U	H	E	L	G	L	O	R	T	N	O	C	L	L	A	B
T	H	E	B	E	A	U	T	I	F	U	L	G	A	M	E	S	P	T	T

SOCCER **SEARCH**

Ball Control
Bicycle Kick
Boot it
Brace
Clean Sheet
Clinical Finisher
Cruyff Turn
Cup-tied
Dead-ball Specialist
Dribbling
Flip Flap
Fox in the Box
Gaffer
Giant-killing
Golden Goal
Hard Man
Hit the Woodwork
Magic Sponge
Man On
Nutmeg
Rainbow Kick
Skipper
Target Man
The Beautiful Game
Treble

ANSWERS ON PAGE 62

CLASSIC FANTASTIC

There are five Captain Canaries hiding in the crowd as Norwich fans celebrate promotion to the Premier League in 2004.

Can you find him?

ANSWERS ON PAGE 62

DESIGN A KIT

Have a go at creating next season's home kit for the Canaries!

MILOT
RASHICA
LOTUS

The Canaries' unique yellow and green colours have been a long held tradition at Carrow Road.

However, excitement and anticipation still surrounds the launch of every new Norwich City kit.

Each and every playing strip forms its own part of Norwich City history and supporters young and old will all have their own favourites. Let's take a look back at four of the best...

1981/82

The Canaries joined forces with kit manufacturer adidas for the production of the club's 1981/82 playing strip and saw City strut their stuff in a classic adidas pinstripe shirt across the next three seasons.

The yellow shirt with green pinstripes carried the trademark three adidas stripes down the sleeves and also had a stylish green collar. In an era before shirt sponsorship was commonplace, the club crest and manufacturer's logo were situated on the chest of the shirt. The green shorts had a large yellow panel down the sides which then carried three green adidas stripes. An all-yellow sock was emblazoned with three green stripes on the top.

This was of course also the first Norwich City kit to carry a shirt sponsorship when the club linked up with Poll Withey Windows during the 1983/84 campaign.

DRESSED TO IMPRESS

Fans of a certain age still regard this strip as one of the best produced for the club. Winning matches certainly helps shape supporters' views on the playing kit and Norwich City enjoyed an excellent 1981/82 season. After suffering relegation from the top flight for the second time in the club's history, City kept faith with manager Ken Brown and he guided the club to an instant return to the First Division in 1981/82 when they secured promotion together with Luton Town and Watford.

HE WORE IT WELL

The return to Carrow Road of Martin O'Neill in February 1982 was the undisputed catalyst for the Canaries' late surge to promotion in 1981/82. City were eleventh in the Second Division when O'Neill returned from Manchester City but once he donned a yellow shirt again, City never looked back and won ten of their final 12 games to land the third and final promotion slot.

1984/85

Norwich City took a giant step into the unknown when kit manufacturer Hummell produced their 1984/85 playing kit and introduced two slightly different shades of yellow to the club's shirt.

This new look gave the shirts a slight striped appearance to them while maintaining the traditional canary yellow. The sleeves carried the manufacturer's arrow-style branding in green together with a green collar. The club crest and Hummell logo were both on the front of the shirt plus the club sponsor, Poll Withey whose name was displayed in a standout red.

The two-tone yellow shirt theme was continued with the shorts which had a green stripe effect created with two shades of green. The Hummell arrows were added to the side of the shorts in yellow together with the manufacturer's logo. The all-yellow socks were enhanced with two of the smart Hummell arrows in green at the top.

DRESSED TO IMPRESS

Another kit in which the Canaries enjoyed great success. This was of course the strip that Ken Brown's side wore throughout their triumphant 1984/85 League Cup winning campaign. There were slight amends made to the shirt for the Wembley final with Sunderland, the Poll Withey logo becoming black rather than red and the words Milk Cup Final 1985 printed above the club crest on the shirt.

HE WORE IT WELL

Steve Bruce soon felt at home wearing this Norwich kit having joined the club from Gillingham in the summer of 1984. He headed home the all-important winning goal in the League Cup semi-final against Ipswich Town before producing a Man of the Match performance in the Wembley final victory over Sunderland.

CHAMPIONSHIP WINNERS 2020/21

Norwich City recorded the club's best points total on the way to winning the Sky Bet Championship title last season.

After a slow start, a Jordan Hugill penalty away at Rotherham got the Canaries up and running and they didn't look back from that moment. A run of five wins and two draws from the following seven games got Norwich to top spot by the late November.

December was then a fruitful month with Josh Martin and Jacob Sørensen getting their first goals for the club in victories over Sheffield Wednesday and Nottingham Forest, before Teemu Pukki netted in victories over Blackburn Rovers and Reading.

The good form continued into the new year, with Grant Hanley heading home in a 2-1 win away at Cardiff City and Hugill getting a double in a win against Bristol City, but a run of three games without a victory rocked Norwich City's progress and saw the lead, the club had built up over the chasing pack, shrink.

The Championship and promotion back to the Premier League was effectively won in the games that followed though, with nine straight victories recorded. A stunning 7-0 victory over Huddersfield Town was perhaps the pinnacle of the campaign, in early April, with Pukki netting a hat-trick in that match. A 1-0 win over Derby then put the club on the verge of a return to the Premier League, which was then confirmed hours before the players took to the pitch against Bournemouth, by results elsewhere.

Norwich then secured the title with a 4-1 win over Reading at Carrow Road, which saw several supporters turn up to the ground to celebrate with the players after the final whistle.

BACK WHERE WE BELONG

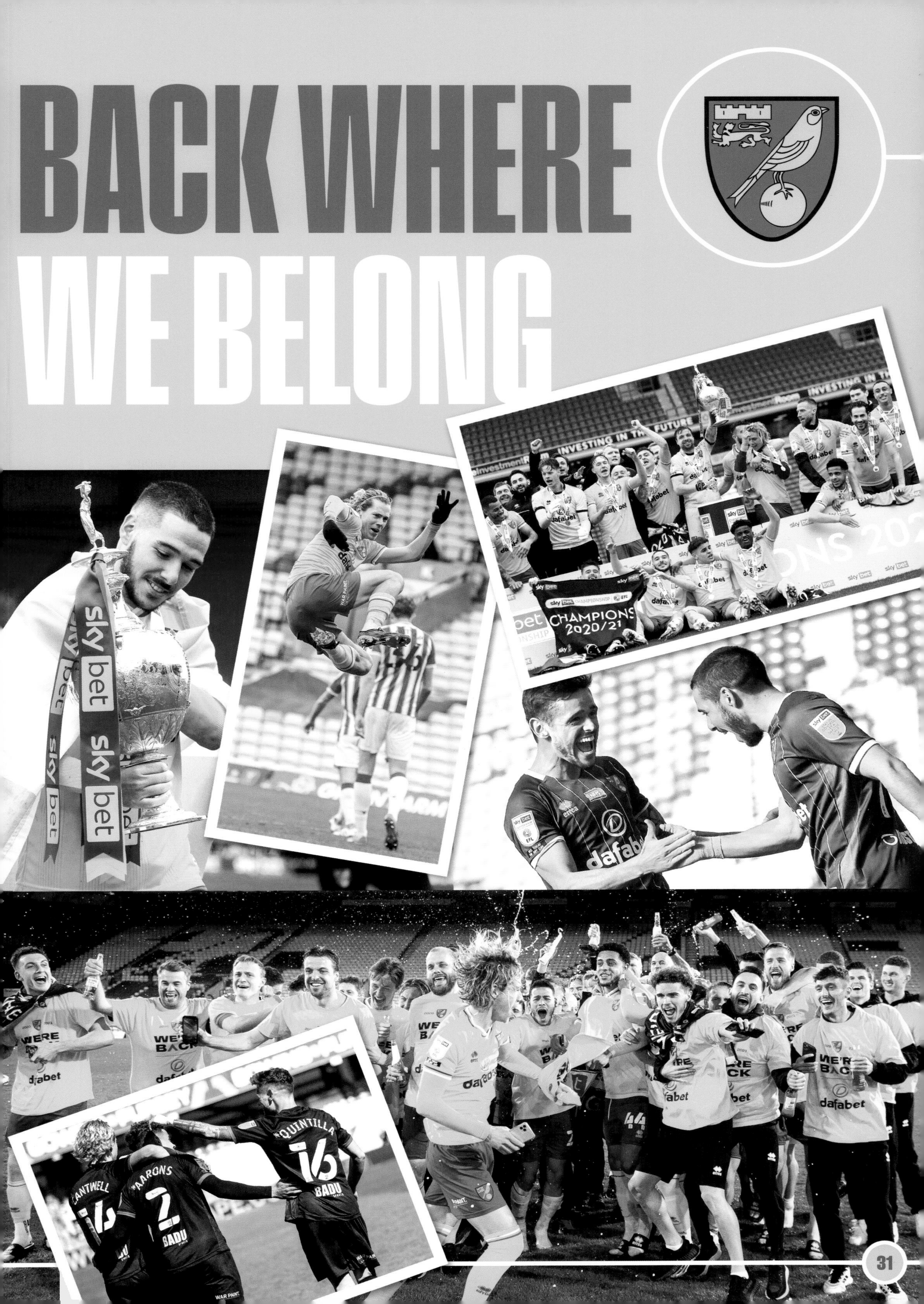

PIERRE
LEES-MELOU
LOTUS

It has been said that dribbling is a dying art. The pace of the modern game makes it more difficult, but there are players about, even in today's lightning fast conditions, who have the confidence to keep hold of the ball and take on defenders.

DRIBBLING

SOCCER SKILLS

EXERCISE ONE

As a warm-up exercise, players A and B each dribble a ball around a 20 x 10m grid, avoiding each other, but staying within the grid boundary lines.

They progress to a 'cat and mouse' race between the corners - the player with the most visits to each corner wins the race. One of the main problems in this exercise is avoiding the other player, and their ball.

EXERCISE TWO

Now for a more realistic exercise. Six players are used as shown, with three attackers and three defenders at any one time. When play starts, the players with the ball attack any of the three opposing goals, changing their target as they choose. The defenders have, simply, to stop their opposite number from scoring, but must not interfere with any other pair.

Key Factors

1. **Close control.**
2. **Quick change of direction.**
3. **Acceleration away from defender.**
4. **Feints, to wrong-foot defender.**
5. **Head up to see the whole picture.**

When the defenders win possession, they become the attackers, and go for goal themselves. This can be a very enjoyable practice, but also quite tiring.

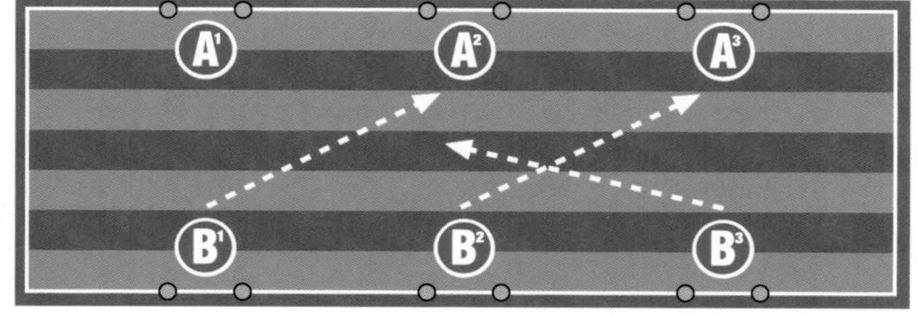

1
ANSWER
2
1932
ANSWER
3
ANSWER
4
ANSWER
5
ANSWER

GUESS
THE CLUB
6
ANSWER
7
EST·1
ANSWER
8
ANSWER
Each football holds the clues to the identity of a Premier League or Football League club, how quickly can you solve them?
9
WOLVES
ANSWER
10
ANSWER
ANSWERS ON PAGE 62
35

GAME OF THE SEASON

NORWICH CITY 7 HUDDERSFIELD TOWN 0

Norwich City went into the home fixture with Huddersfield Town in scintillating form having won nine of the previous eleven matches and drawn the other two.

They also welcomed back Todd Cantwell and Max Aarons to the starting line-up after they had missed the previous match, a 1-1 draw with Preston North End, because of a late return from England Under-21 duty.

It was Cantwell who set up the first goal as he burst into the area from the left, slaloming past two challenges before teeing up Teemu Pukki to side foot home from six yards. On 20 minutes it was 2-0 as Emi Buendía played a ball over the top of the Town defence for Pukki to race clear and fire past Joel Castro Pereira at his near post, before Buendía fired home number three in off the post from outside the box.

Cantwell then fired number four into the top corner and it was 5-0 at half-time as Buendía played a quick one-two with Kieran Dowell in the box to allow the former Everton man to tap home from close range.

The goals slowed a little in the second half, but Pukki still completed his hat-trick from the penalty spot, after the hour when Oliver Skipp ran the length of the field to burst into the opposition box and draw a foul. The scoring was then completed with 12 minutes to go as Aarons sent a low cross that Jordan Hugill side footed home.

GIANNOULIS
30
BUENDIA
17
dafabet
17
dafabet
9

Wales international striker Iwan Roberts scored an impressive 96 goals for the Canaries between 1997 and 2004. Roberts was signed by Mike Walker from Wolves for a fee of £850,000 in the summer of 1997.

Despite a disappointing first season in Norfolk, he went on to become one of the Carrow Road crowd's all-time favourite players.

He was twice voted Player of the Season and won a place in the inaugural Hall of Fame during the 2002 Centenary celebrations. Iwan captained City in their 2001/02 Play-Off final against Birmingham at the Millennium Stadium and also chipped in with vital goals during the 2003/04 Nationwide First Division title-winning campaign.

CANARIES HEROES

IWAN ROBERTS

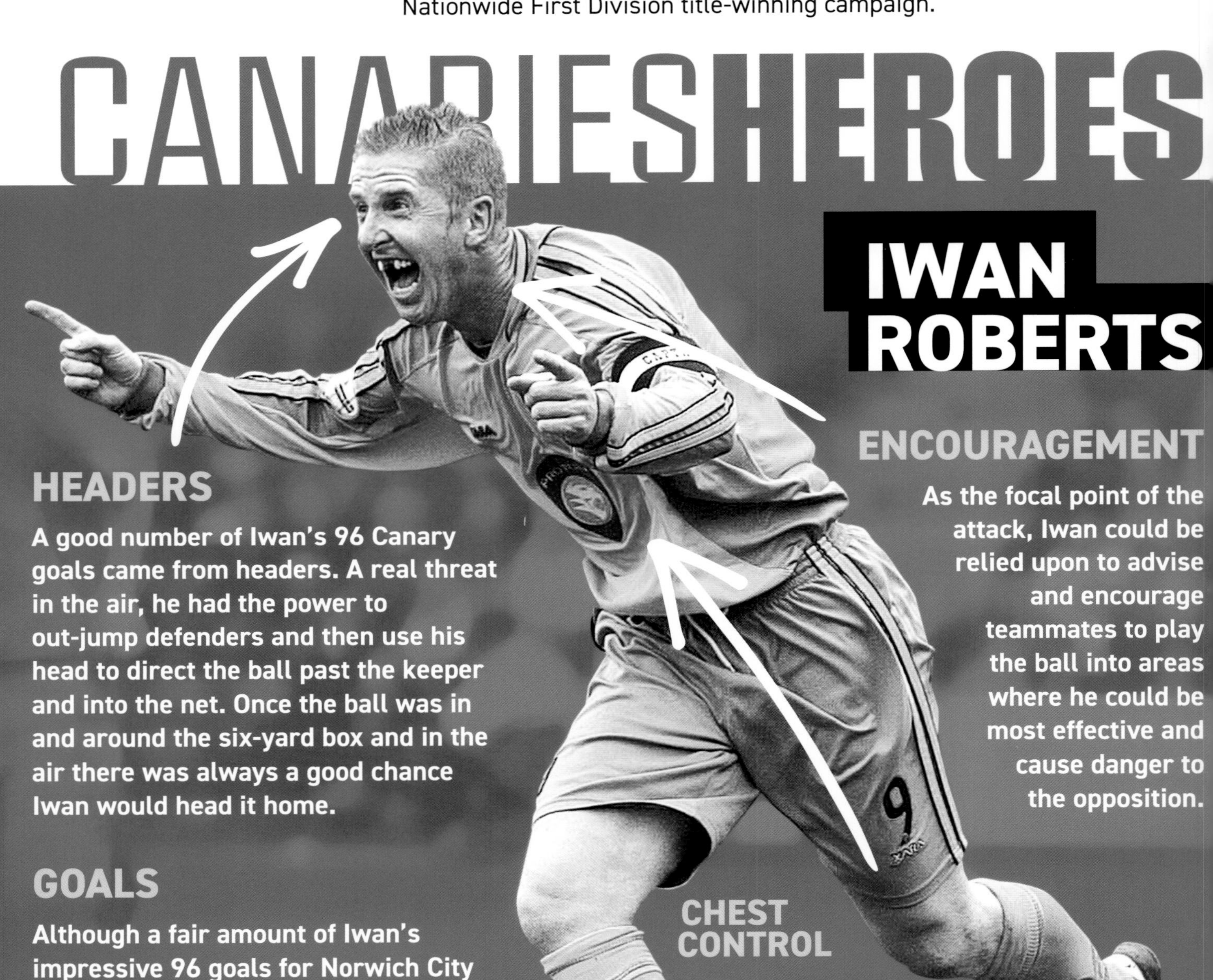

HEADERS

A good number of Iwan's 96 Canary goals came from headers. A real threat in the air, he had the power to out-jump defenders and then use his head to direct the ball past the keeper and into the net. Once the ball was in and around the six-yard box and in the air there was always a good chance Iwan would head it home.

GOALS

Although a fair amount of Iwan's impressive 96 goals for Norwich City came from headers, he was pretty lethal with a trusty right foot too. With the ability to take shots first time and confidently dispatch penalties too - when Iwan pulled the trigger with his right foot it rarely let him down.

ENCOURAGEMENT

As the focal point of the attack, Iwan could be relied upon to advise and encourage teammates to play the ball into areas where he could be most effective and cause danger to the opposition.

CHEST CONTROL

As a strong centre-forward who led the Norwich City attack so well, Iwan was blessed with a great ability to play with his back to goal and take the ball under control on his chest. He could then hold up play while others arrived in support or lay the ball off to a teammate.

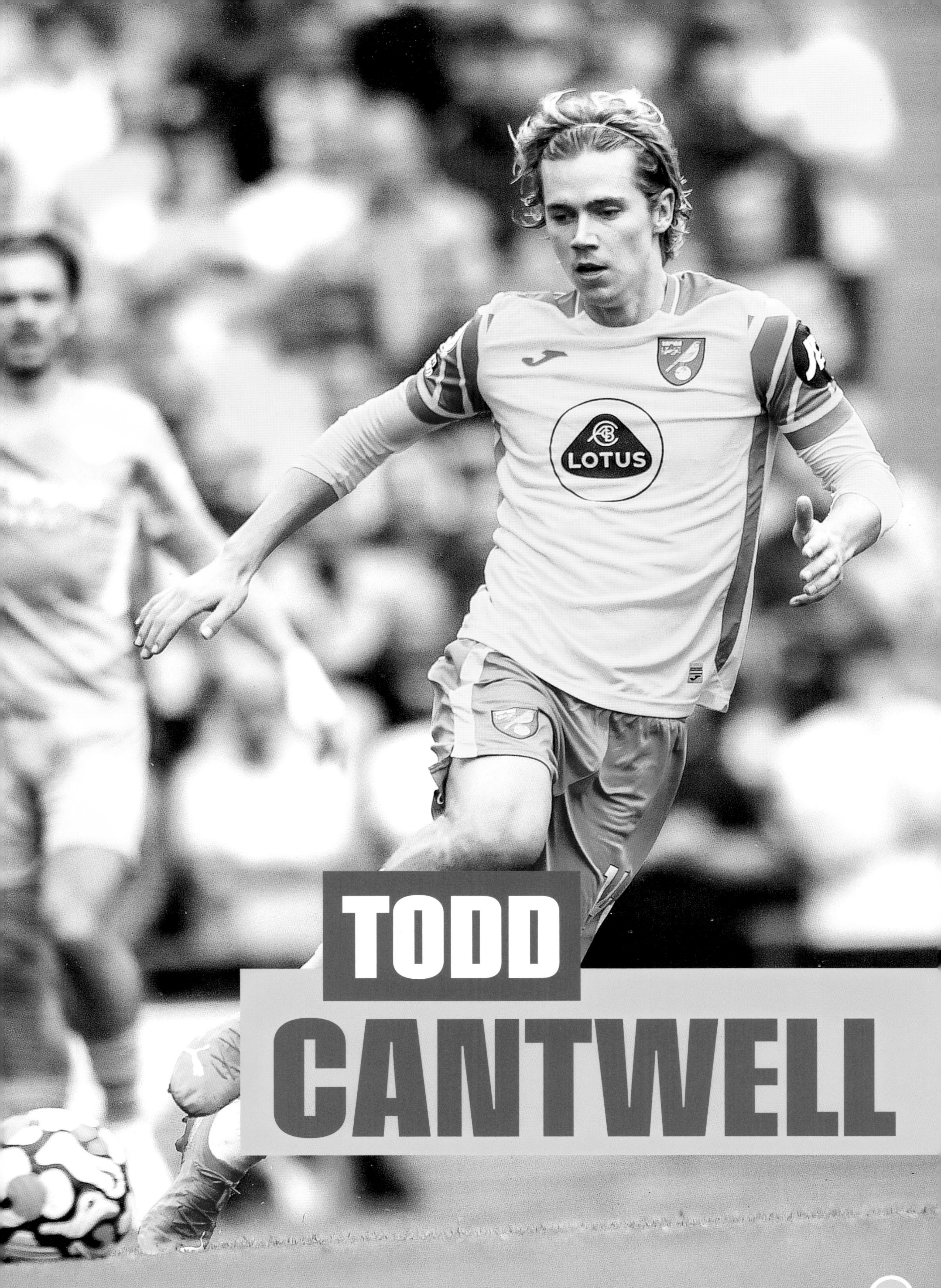

TODD CANTWELL

RECORD APPEARANCE MAKER

Legendary goalkeeper Kevin Keelan proudly holds the record as the Canaries' top appearance maker having played a colossal 673 times for the club between 1963 and 1980.

A vital member of the 1971/72 promotion-winning team, Kevin also made two appearances for City at Wembley in the League Cup finals of 1973 and 1975. Voted Player of the Season in 1972/73 and again in 1973/74, Kevin is a member of the club's Hall of Fame. His spectacular saves and bravery made him a much-admired character with both supporters in the stands and teammates in the dressing room.

He remains an extremely popular visitor whenever he returns to Carrow Road from his current home in Florida. Kevin attended the club's 'Greatest Ever' event in May 2008 when he was officially confirmed as Norwich City's greatest-ever goalkeeper.

YOUNGEST PLAYER

Striker Kris Renton progressed though the Canaries' Academy to become the youngest-ever player to appear in the club's first team. The teenage Scot made history when he replaced Lee Croft in the final minute of City's 2-1 Championship victory away to Leicester City on Saturday, April 14, 2007.

Kris was aged just 16 years 276 days old when he made his debut and his appearance saw him supersede Ryan Jarvis as Norwich City's youngest player. It was a close call though, with Kris being just six days younger than Jarvis was when he faced Walsall on April 19, 2003 aged 16 years 282 days.

Under the management of Peter Grant, Kris made three first-team appearances for City before his progress was disrupted by injury later in 2007.

After returning to fitness, Kris was loaned to King's Lynn and Brechin City before returning north of the border permanently where he has plied his trade in Scotland's lower divisions.

TOP GOALSCORER

Ace marksman Johnny Gavin holds the record as Norwich City's record goalscorer. In two separate spells with the club between 1949 to 1954 and 1955 to 1958, Johnny made a total of 338 appearances and found the back of the opposition's net on 132 occasions.

Along with Terry Allcock, who netted 127 goals for the club, Johnny is therefore one of only two men to have reached three figures in the goals stakes for the Canaries.

Despite a lack of height, surprisingly a great deal of his goals came from headers and it is extremely unlikely that his 132-goal haul will ever be overtaken. A member of the club's Hall of Fame, Johnny died in Cambridgeshire on September 18, 2007.

RECORD MAKERS

A selection of players, games, facts and figures which all shape the club's proud history.

Former captain and fans' favourite Russell Martin is Norwich City's record appearance maker in the Premier League with 125 games.

Russell joined Norwich City, initially on loan, from Peterborough United in 2009, and scored his first goal for the club in a 3-1 defeat to Doncaster Rovers with a diving header on September 14, 2010.

He helped the club to back-to-back promotions in his first two seasons at the club. In the Championship campaign of 2010/11, he played 49 games and scored five goals from his defensive position and finished as the runner up in the club's fan-voted player of the season award. Three seasons in the Premier League followed and he was officially named club captain on August 10, 2013. He would achieve another promotion with Norwich in the 2014/15 season when he played 48 games in the Sky Bet Championship as the club won promotion via the play-offs.

RECORD PREMIER LEAGUE APPEARANCE MAKER

As we all know there are few better places to be than inside a packed Carrow Road and cheering Daniel Farke's team on to victory.

The current capacity at today's modern all-seater Carrow Road is 27,329 and knowing what Carrow Road is like with 27,000-plus fans inside, just stop and think what it must have been like when a whopping 43,984 were crammed inside to witness the Canaries' FA Cup quarter-final match with Leicester City in March 1963.

Following the Canaries' FA Cup heroics in 1958/59 when they reached the semi-final, the city of Norwich was once again gripped by cup fever come March 30, 1963 when the ground's record attendance was recorded for this quarter-final tie. Second Division Norwich had dispatched Blackpool, Newcastle United, and Manchester City but despite being backed by this bumper crowd, could not find a way past the Foxes' England goalkeeper Gordon Banks as the visitors proceeded to the semi-final with a 2-0 victory.

RECORD ATTENDANCE

Head coach Daniel Farke signed a four-year contract at the club at the start of the season, keeping him here until the summer of 2025.

To celebrate this, we are going to test your knowledge of the boss.

Daniel's first game as Norwich City head coach ended in a 1-1 draw against which London team?

1.

Where did Daniel begin his managerial career?

2.

Who was Norwich City's top goalscorer in Daniel's first season as head coach?

3.

Norwich City finished as champions in the Sky Bet Championship in Daniel's second season in charge, but how many points did the team get that season?

4.

Which player did Daniel give a debut to in the 2018/19 season in the East Anglian derby?

5.

How old is Daniel Farke?

6.

Who was Daniel Farke's first signing as Norwich City manager?

7.

Which Premier League manager, and friend of Daniel Farke, said he likes to watch Norwich in his free time?

8.

There are only two other German managers in the Premier League, can you name them?

9.

Daniel Farke's first win as a Premier League manager came against which club?

10.

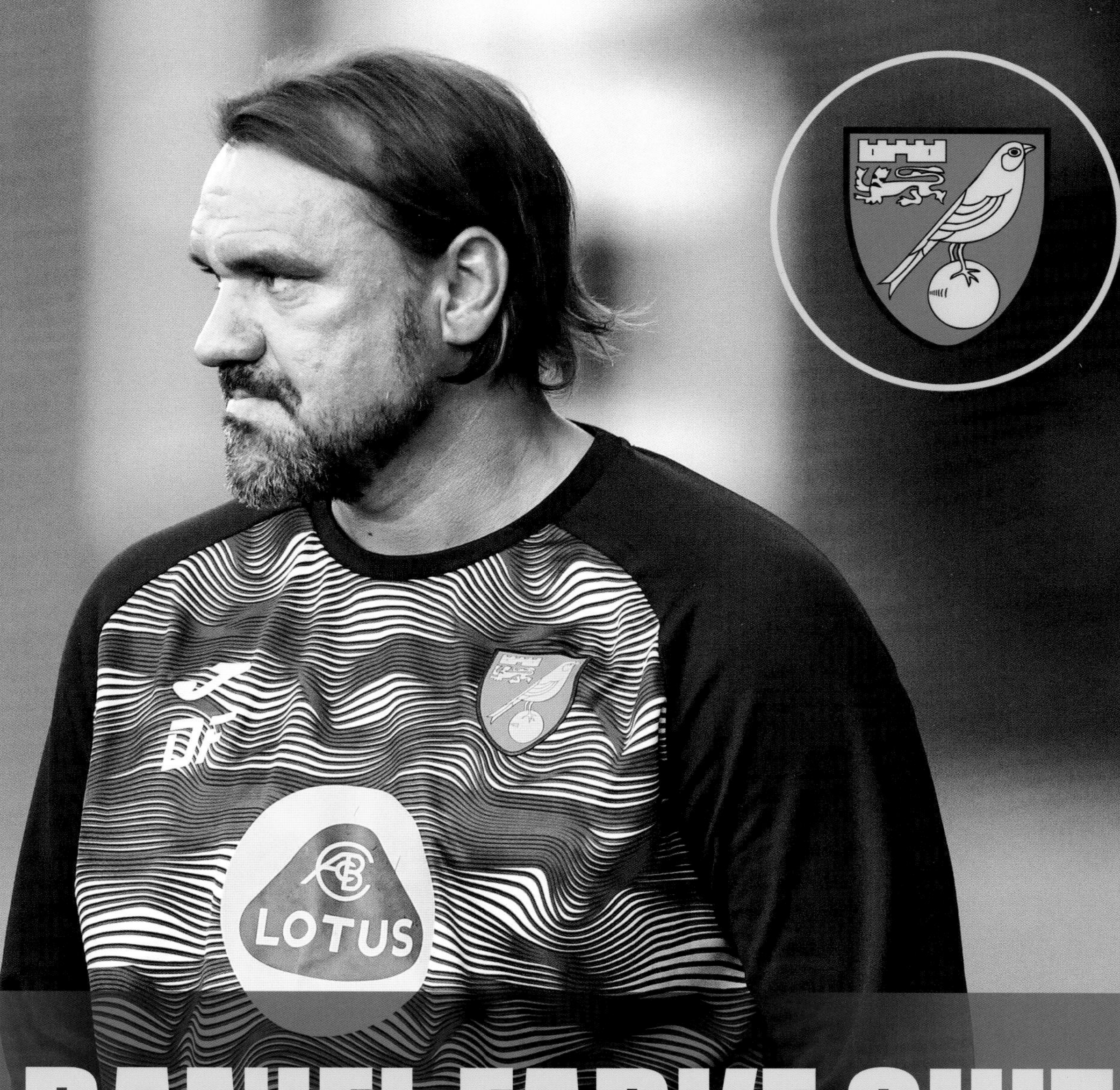

THE DANIEL FARKE QUIZ

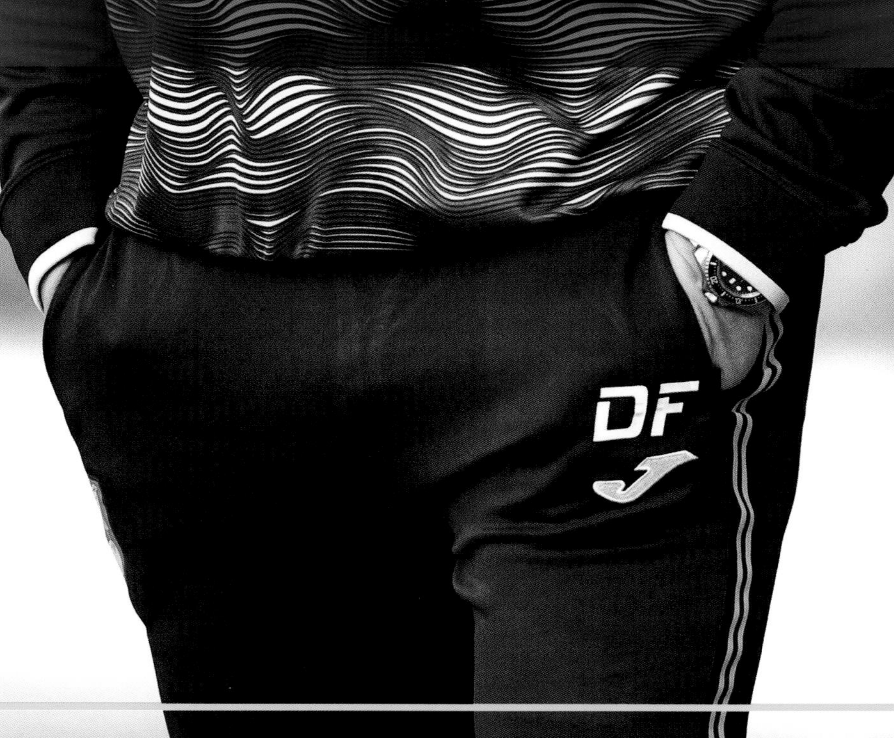

ANSWERS ON PAGE 62

KIERAN
DOWELL

Captain of the Canaries' 2003/04 Nationwide First Division title-winning side, long-serving left-back Adam Drury joined Norwich City in March 2001 from Peterborough United.

Signed by Nigel Worthington, Adam went on to enjoy eleven seasons at Carrow Road while amassing over 350 games for the club. He was an extremely reliable and consistent defender who excelled in one-on-one situations. His polished performances in 2002/03 saw him voted player of the season.

Adam's time at Carrow Road was certainly eventful as he experienced three promotions, two relegations and a play-off final. His loyalty to the Canary cause was rewarded with a testimonial match against Scottish giants Celtic in May 2012.

CANARIES HEROES

ADAM DRURY

RALLYING CALL

Handed the captain's armband by Nigel Worthington, Adam's ability to lead and inspire his teammates was there for all to see. Always there with an encouraging call to those around him, Adam led by example but was never afraid to let players know if standards had dropped.

PASSING SKILLS

Always comfortable with the ball at his feet, Adam was an accomplished ball-playing full-back who could always be relied upon to bring the ball out of defence and help the side turn defence to attack. He built an excellent partnership on the Norwich left with Darren Huckerby playing in front of him.

TEMPERAMENT

Often faced with containing tricky wingers, Adam had the perfect mindset for defending. He very rarely lost concentration and always kept his cool. In the heat of any on-field duel, Adam kept his mind on the task in hand and more often than not came out on top in one-on-one situations.

QUICK ON HIS HEELS

Adam was always alive and alert to danger and when it occurred he was quick on his heels to track and tackle opponents. Not only was he swift over the ground but he was also quick to leap and win headed duels too.

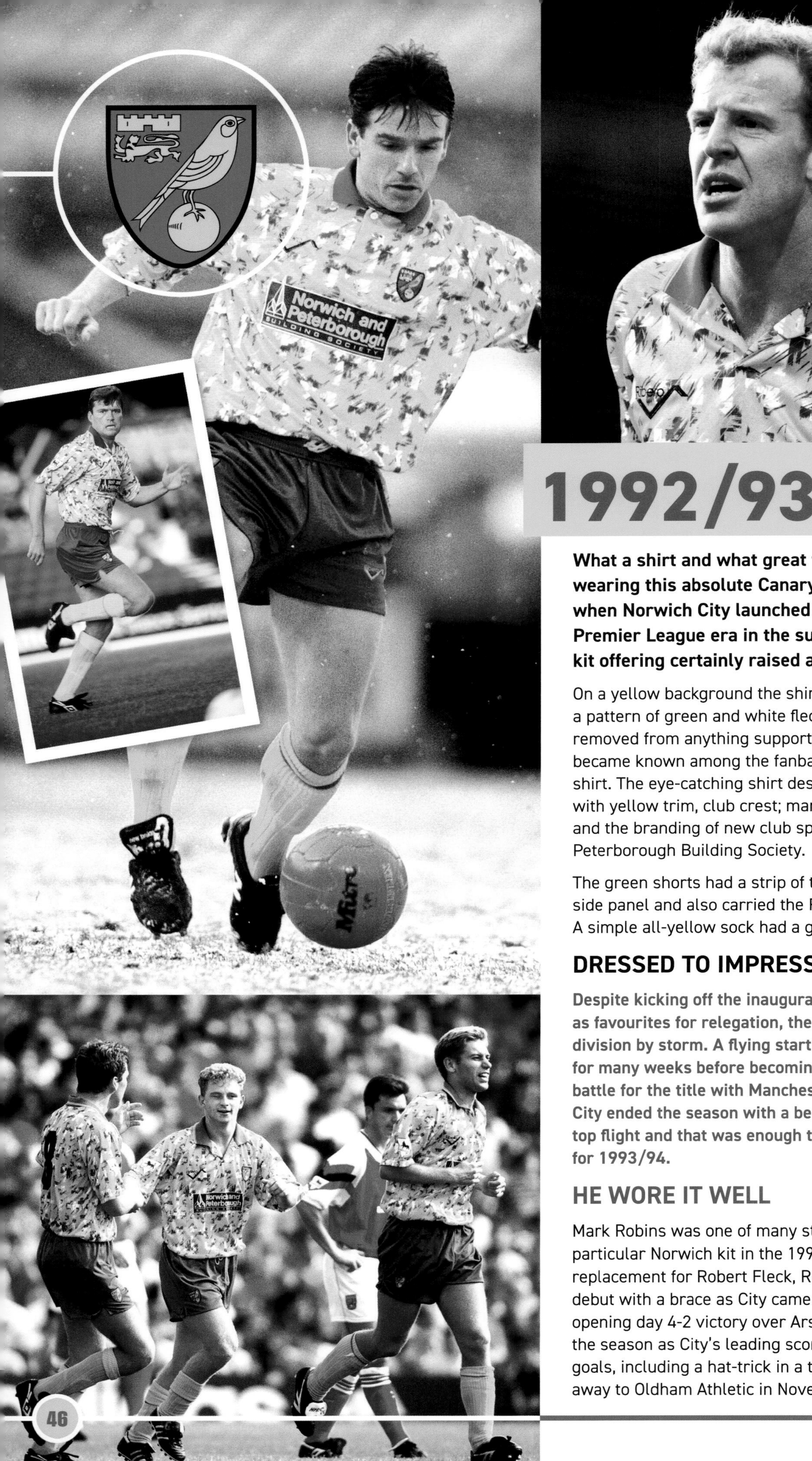

1992/93

What a shirt and what great times Norwich City had wearing this absolute Canary classic. Suffice to say, when Norwich City launched their new-look for the Premier League era in the summer of 1992 the latest kit offering certainly raised a few eyebrows!

On a yellow background the shirt was emblazoned with a pattern of green and white flecks. It was a long way removed from anything supporters had seen before and became known among the fanbase as the 'egg and cress' shirt. The eye-catching shirt design also had a green collar with yellow trim, club crest; manufacturer Ribero's logo and the branding of new club sponsor, Norwich and Peterborough Building Society.

The green shorts had a strip of the shirt design down the side panel and also carried the Ribero logo and club crest. A simple all-yellow sock had a green trim at the top.

DRESSED TO IMPRESS

Despite kicking off the inaugural Premier League season as favourites for relegation, the Canaries took the new division by storm. A flying start saw them lead the table for many weeks before becoming embroiled in a three-way battle for the title with Manchester United and Aston Villa. City ended the season with a best-ever finish of third in the top flight and that was enough to secure European football for 1993/94.

HE WORE IT WELL

Mark Robins was one of many star performers in this particular Norwich kit in the 1992/93 season. Signed as replacement for Robert Fleck, Robins marked his Norwich debut with a brace as City came from 2-0 down to record an opening day 4-2 victory over Arsenal at Highbury. He ended the season as City's leading scorer with 15 Premier League goals, including a hat-trick in a thrilling 3-2 televised win away to Oldham Athletic in November 1992.

A shirt which was worn by many of the thousands of Canary fans that travelled to Wembley for the 2014/15 Play-Off final victory over Middlesbrough, this kit is another that brings fond memories flooding back.

2014/15

The fourth strip that was produced for City by Italian kit manufacturer Errea, this shirt had a different look as it moved away from the traditional style of a predominantly yellow shirt. With a large green panel at the top of the shirt, the chest area had a yellow v-neck and a green collar. The top green panel also housed the club crest and Errea logo with the sponsors branding appearing in the larger yellow area below.

The green shorts had an attractive yellow trim while the socks replicated the shirt style with a large green section at the top. The socks also had the manufacturer's logo and club initials 'NCFC' stitched into them.

DRESSED TO IMPRESS

A memorable season at Carrow Road as Norwich returned to the Premier League at the first time of asking after a third-place finish and a successful Play-Off campaign. After doubling local rivals Ipswich Town in the regulation season, the Canaries also defeated Town in the Play-Off semi-final en route to promotion. The sight of Nathan Redmond jumping for joy in this kit after restoring City's semi-final lead is an iconic Canary moment.

HE WORE IT WELL

Midfield general Bradley Johnson certainly saved some of his best Norwich performances for this kit. He netted an incredible 15 goals from midfield including an absolute rocket to open the scoring in the East Anglian derby victory over Ipswich Town at Carrow Road in March 2015. He ended the campaign as a Wembley winner and the Canaries' Player of the Season.

ALL KITTED OUT

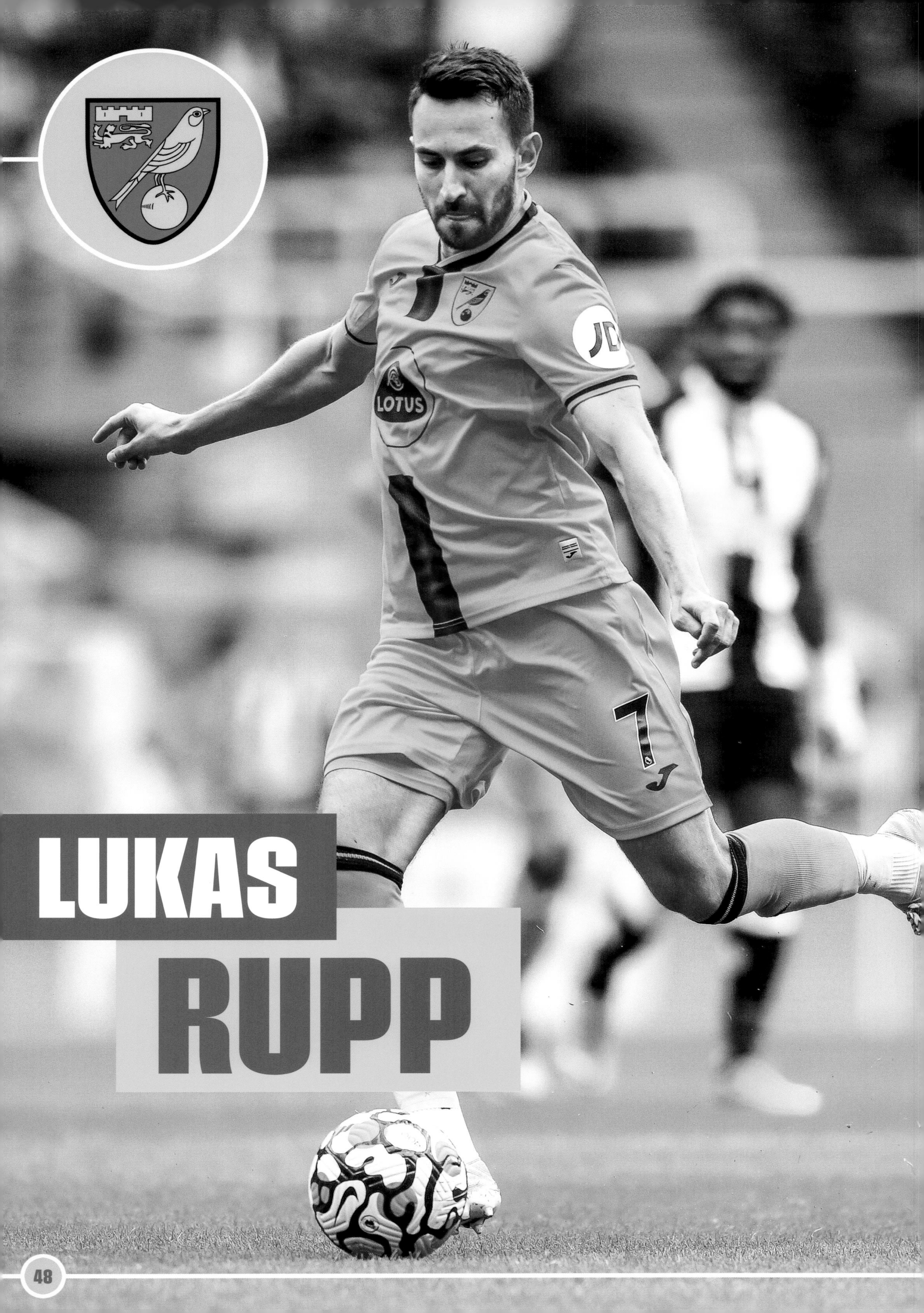
LOTUS
7
LUKAS
RUPP

One of a player's greatest assets is the ability to win the ball. The following exercise can be used to improve a player's tackling abilities.

TACKLING

SOCCER SKILLS

EXERCISE

Set up a 10m x 20m grid.

In this two-on-two exercise, the aim of the game is to score a goal by taking the ball past the two opposing defenders, to the end line, and stand on the ball. The defenders just have to stop them.

As well as producing plenty of opportunities for the defenders to tackle, this session will test the defenders' abilities to work together, and communicate.

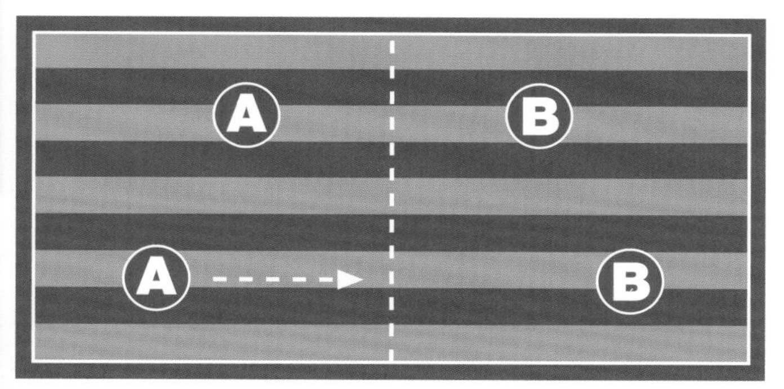

Key Factors

1. **Be patient - do not dive in.**
2. **Stay on your feet if possible.**
3. **Time the tackle with bodyweight behind it.**
4. **Be determined to win it.**

The reason that great players win so many tackles is not just because they know how to tackle and have good technique, it is because they have big hearts and are determined to win their challenges on the pitch.

ODDBALLS

Three of the four pictures in each football represent a Premier League or Football League club, can you figure out the football club as well as the odd one out?

ANSWERS ON PAGE 62

6
A
B
C
D
1905
ANSWER
7
A
B
C
D
ANSWER
8
A
B
C
D
ANSWER
9
A
B
C
D
FOOTBALL CLUB
ANSWER
10
A
B
C
D
ANSWER

PLAYER OF THE SEASON

Following a truly sensational season for the Canaries in the 2020/21 Sky Bet Championship title-winning campaign there were many contenders for the club's player of the season award.

Voted for by the fans it is a prestigious award, with the winner being given the Barry Butler Memorial Trophy, which is named in memory of one of our former captains.

The voting for the accolade was close and competitive, with Finnish international Teemu Pukki, who scored 26 goals in 42 matches, not even getting a place in the top three.

Third place went to Oliver Skipp, who had joined the club the previous summer on a season-long loan from Tottenham Hotspur. Skipp was a revelation in the City side, injecting energy and tough tackling to the Canaries' midfield as his workrate helped the club to a much-improved defensive record in the 2020/21 season.

He played 45 games in total for Norwich, scoring his first professional goal in an away victory over Birmingham City, and finishing with a pass completion rate of 88 per cent across his games for the club. It is of no surprise to anyone at Norwich City to see the youngster now performing well in the Tottenham first team this campaign.

Second on the list was Grant Hanley. It is the second time the Scottish defender has been runner up for Norwich City in the player of the season award, after he finished behind James Maddison in the 2017/18 campaign.

Hanley showcased his quality across 40 games for Norwich, beating any Championship striker in a footrace and scoring a crucial goal away at Cardiff City. His defensive intelligence contributed to a much-improved clean sheet record for Norwich, with 33 goals against being the second fewest in the division.

However, going forward, Norwich City were equally impressive and a large part of that came down to the brilliance of Emi Buendía who became the first South American to win the Barry Butler Memorial Player of the Season trophy for us.

Buendía finished the campaign with 16 assists and 15 goals and on the back of that received his first call up to the Argentina squad for their World Cup qualifying matches with Chile and Colombia in June.

MALAYSIA
BERJAYA
dafabet
19
5
20
BoyleSports
SWALLOW

MAX AARONS

COLOUR PRZEMYSŁAW PŁACHETA

GUESS WHO

1. WHO AM I?

I joined the Canaries in 2012

Chris Hughton was the Norwich manager that signed me

I marked my Norwich City debut with a goal in a cup tie

I scored a notable winning goal in a match at Old Trafford

I won promotion with Norwich on three occasions

3. WHO AM I?

I began my playing career in the Norwich City youth team

My father also played for Norwich City

I made my debut when Dave Stringer was Norwich manager

I scored 25 Premier League goals for Norwich City in 1993/94

After leaving Carrow Road I was a Premier League winner

2. WHO AM I?

I joined the Canaries in 2016

Early in my Norwich career I was loaned to a Scottish team

My first league goal for Norwich came against Preston North End

I was voted City's Player of the Season in 2017/18

After leaving Norwich City I have won full international caps with England

Can you identify these six former Canaries from the clues given? Good luck!

I joined Norwich City in the summer of 2009

I netted a hat-trick in just my second competitive game for the club

I was leading scorer in Norwich's 2009/10 League One title triumph

I netted a very special hat-trick at Carrow Road in November 2010

Since retiring from football I have tried my hand at wrestling

4. WHO AM I?

I was born in Solihull

I made my Canary debut back in 1981

I marked my Norwich debut with a goal

I was the club's leading scorer in the successful 1985 League Cup triumph

I later returned to Carrow Road as assistant manager and then manager

5. WHO AM I?

6. WHO AM I?

I began my career with Lincoln City

I initially arrived at Norwich City on loan

My first Norwich City goal came against Stoke City

Norwich won promotion to the Premier League in my first season at Carrow Road

I was twice voted the club's Player of the Season

ANSWERS ON PAGE 62

A real Carrrow Road favourite, Wes Hoolahan was a great servant who enjoyed many ups and downs in a Canary career that experienced three promotions and three relegations. He boasted a wonderful stat of never losing a local derby during his 352-game Canary career.

A talented playmaker, he starred under Paul Lambert and was also a member of City's 2014/15 play-off winning team. Initially recruited by Glenn Roeder from Blackpool in 2008, the Republic of Ireland international went on to become the Canaries' most capped player.

The final home game of the 2017/18 season saw the curtain fall on Wes' ten-year stay at Carrow Road as the fans' favourite signed off in style with a goal in a 2-1 victory over Leeds United.

CANARIES HEROES

WES HOOLAHAN

EYE FOR AN OPENING

Not only was Wes extremely comfortable on the ball but he also showed great vision and awareness on the pitch. He appeared to have the perfect eye for a quick pass to help the Canaries mount another attack.

QUICK FEET

Naturally blessed with exceptional close control and dribbling skills, Wes had the ability to jinx his way past opponents and into dangerous areas. Always indentified as the dangerman, Wes proved to be a tricky player for opposition to get to grips with.

INTELLIGENCE

A player's football intelligence is often spoken about and Wes had it in abundance. He had the skill of making time on the ball, orchestrating the pattern of play and playing creative forward balls. He also had that ability of knowing the runs a teammate would make and the ability to find them with the minimum of fuss.

ADVICE

In his latter years at Carrow Road, Wes used his experience and knowledge gained from playing at the top level for club and country to help the younger players in the Norwich team.

GRANT
HANLEY
LOTUS
captain

Can you guess which countries the following Norwich City players play for from the following clues?

WHERE AM I FROM?

1. CHRISTOS TZOLIS & DIMITRIS GIANNOULIS

Our country is considered to birthplace of democracy. It is also the place where the first Olympic Games were held and is famous for feta cheese.

2. TIM KRUL

I play for a small European country, which is famous for tulips and windmills and because it is very flat everyone cycles. My country has finished runners up in the World Cup on three occasions in 1974, 1978 and 2010.

3. TEEMU PUKKI

My country is famous for being the happiest country in the world. It is located near Sweden, Denmark and Norway, but is a Nordic country not Scandinavian.

5. JOSH SARGENT

At international level I play for one of the most famous countries in the world, which is famous for places like the Grand Canyon, Hollywood and the Golden Gate bridge.

4. BILLY GILMOUR, KENNY MCLEAN & GRANT HANLEY

Our country qualified for Euro 2020, the first major tournament we have reached since 1998. Our country is famous for its beautiful landscapes, castles and lochs.

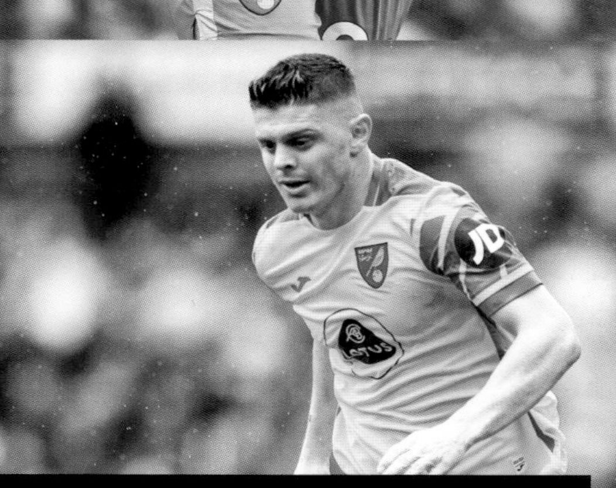

6. MILOT RASHICA

My country is the second youngest country in the world, having declared its independence from Serbia in 2008. It's capital is Pristina and the country is located to the north of North Macedonia.

7. MATHIAS NORMANN

I play for a country which is known as the Land of the Midnight Sun. It is famous for its phenomenal fjords, lakes and magical skies. You can see the Northern Lights from the northern part of this country.

8. OZAN KABAK

A play for a country which is known as the gateway to Asia. With the black sea to the north, my country has borders with Greece and Bulgaria to the west and Iran and Armenia to the east.

ANSWERS ON PAGE 62

ANSWERS

PAGE 23 · SOCCER SEARCH

Bicycle Kick.

PAGE 24 · CLASSIC FANTASTIC

PAGE 34 · GUESS THE CLUB

1. Newcastle United. 2. Wigan Athletic. 3. Leeds United. 4. Charlton Athletic. 5. Coventry City. 6. AFC Wimbledon. 7. Liverpool. 8. Millwall. 9. Wolverhampton Wanderers. 10. Nottingham Forest.

PAGE 42 · THE DANIEL FARKE QUIZ

1. Fulham. 2. SV Lippstadt. 3. James Maddison. 4. 94pts. 5. Max Aarons. 6. 44. 7. Marley Watkins. 8. Pep Guardiola. 9. Thomas Tuchel and Jürgen Klopp. 10. Newcastle United.

PAGE 50 · ODD BALLS

1. Sunderland, C. 2. Portsmouth, C. 3. Arsenal, B. 4. Crewe Alexandra, A. 5. Queens Park Rangers, C. 6. Crystal Palace, B. 7. Tottenham Hotspur, B. 8. Reading, B. 9. Birmingham City, C. 10. West Ham United, D.

PAGE 56 · GUESS WHO?

1. Alex Tettey. 2. James Maddison. 3. Chris Sutton. 4. Grant Holt. 5. John Deehan. 6. Darren Huckerby.

PAGE 60 · WHERE AM I FROM?

1. Greece. 2. Netherlands. 3. Finland. 4. Scotland. 5. USA. 6. Kosovo. 7. Norway. 8. Turkey.